Canada's
LAND & PEOPLE

NOVA SCOTIA

Harry Beckett

Weigl

CALGARY
www.weigl.com

Published by Weigl Educational Publishers Limited
6325 10 Street SE
Calgary, Alberta   T2H 2Z9

Website: www.weigl.com
Copyright ©2008 Weigl Educational Publishers Limited

Library and Archives Canada Cataloguing in Publication

Beckett, Harry, 1936-
    Nova Scotia / Harry Beckett.

(Canada's land and people)
Includes index.
ISBN 978-1-55388-359-3 (bound)
ISBN 978-1-55388-360-9 (pbk.)

    1. Nova Scotia--Juvenile literature. I. Title. II. Series.
FC2311.2.B435 2007   j971.6   C2007-902203-0

Printed in the United States of America
1 2 3 4 5 6 7 8 9 0 11 10 09 08 07

Every reasonable effort has been made to trace ownership and to obtain permission to reprint copyright material. The publishers would be pleased to have any errors or omissions brought to their attention so that they may be corrected in subsequent printings.

We acknowledge the financial support of the Government of Canada through the Book Publishing Industry Development Program (BPIDP) for our publishing activities.

Photograph credits: Philip S. Neuhoff, University of Florida Department of Geological Sciences: page 11 bottom right; Courtesy of Pier 21 Society: page 17 middle left; ©Province of Nova Scotia. Used with permission: page 15 top left.

Project Coordinator
Heather C. Hudak

Design
Terry Paulhus

All of the Internet URLs given in the book were valid at the time of publication. However, due to the dynamic nature of the Internet, some addresses may have changed, or sites may have ceased to exist since publication. While the author and publisher regret any inconvenience this may cause readers, no responsibility for any such changes can be accepted by either the author or the publisher.

Contents

About Nova Scotia

Nova Scotia joined **Confederation** in 1867. It was among the first Canadian provinces. Today, Nova Scotia covers 55,490 square kilometres of land. It is Canada's second-smallest province after Prince Edward Island.

Nova Scotia is one of Canada's three Maritime Provinces. New Brunswick and Prince Edward Island are the other two Maritime Provinces. Maritime Provinces have water on at least three sides. Only a narrow piece of land links Nova Scotia to mainland Canada.

In 1621, Great Britain's King James I gave land in present-day Canada to Sir William Alexander from Scotland. Alexander named the land *Nova Scotia*, which is Latin for "New Scotland." Many early settlers came to Nova Scotia from Scotland.

Nova Scotia's official **mace** has a crown at the top to honour the province's ties to Great Britain. It was presented to the provincial government in 1930.

ABOUT THE FLAG

In 1625, British King Charles I approved Nova Scotia's shield. The shield is shown on Nova Scotia's flag. The flag's shield has a Royal Lion for Scottish royalty. The blue "X" stands for the Cross of Saint Andrew, Scotland's patron saint. The flag became official in 1929, more than 300 years after it was first designed.

LEGEND

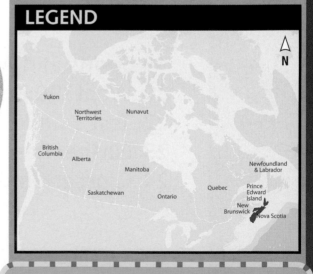

ACTION Draw a flag for your hometown. Use colours to show what is important where you live. Write a paragraph to explain why you chose these colours.

Places to Visit in Nova Scotia

Nova Scotia offers many special places to visit and exciting things to do. This map shows just a few. Where would you like to visit in Nova Scotia? Can you find these places on the map?

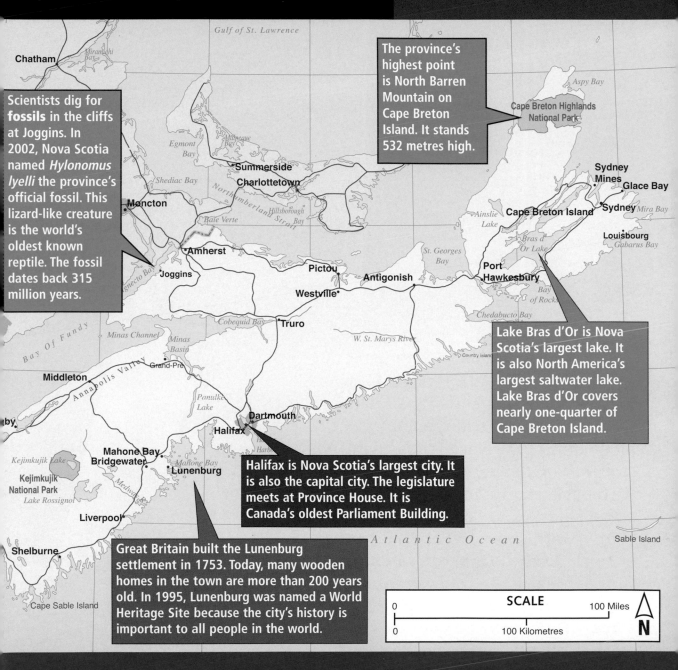

The province's highest point is North Barren Mountain on Cape Breton Island. It stands 532 metres high.

Scientists dig for **fossils** in the cliffs at Joggins. In 2002, Nova Scotia named *Hylonomus lyelli* the province's official fossil. This lizard-like creature is the world's oldest known reptile. The fossil dates back 315 million years.

Lake Bras d'Or is Nova Scotia's largest lake. It is also North America's largest saltwater lake. Lake Bras d'Or covers nearly one-quarter of Cape Breton Island.

Halifax is Nova Scotia's largest city. It is also the capital city. The legislature meets at Province House. It is Canada's oldest Parliament Building.

Great Britain built the Lunenburg settlement in 1753. Today, many wooden homes in the town are more than 200 years old. In 1995, Lunenburg was named a World Heritage Site because the city's history is important to all people in the world.

SCALE

0   100 Miles

0   100 Kilometres

N

Beautiful Landscapes

Every Nova Scotia city and town is located within 56 kilometres of a coast. The Atlantic Upland covers most of Nova Scotia from the Atlantic Ocean westward to the centre. The mountains of the Nova Scotia Highlands stretch from the Bay of Fundy to Cape Breton Island. The Lowlands lie between the uplands. Nova Scotia has mild winters with about 190 centimetres of snow yearly. Warm water from the Gulf of Mexico and cold water from the Arctic Ocean meet off Nova Scotia's shores. These two strong ocean currents create thick sea fog in the late spring. The ocean currents keep summer temperatures cool.

More than 3,000 lakes dot Nova Scotia's landscape. Lake Ainslie on Cape Breton Island is Nova Scotia's largest natural freshwater lake. Lake Ainslie is part of the Atlantic Uplands.

Many rivers, such as the Annapolis, Sissiboo, and Saint Mary's, flow to the ocean from Nova Scotia's Atlantic Uplands.

Nova Scotia has more than 3,000 islands off its rocky coasts. Sable Island lies in the Atlantic Ocean. A herd of wild horses and large colonies of seals live on Sable Island.

The Bay of Fundy brings the world's highest tides to Nova Scotia's shores. More than 100 billion tonnes of sea water rush in and out of the bay twice a day.

Early European settlers built dikes in the Lowlands' coastal marshes. Many **dikes** still work today to control flooding from tides.

Fur, Feathers, and Flowers

Foxes, porcupines, minks, otters, and other small animals live in Nova Scotia. Black bears, Canada lynx, and white-tailed deer live in the forests. Colourful wildflowers, such as wild roses, violets, and water lilies, bloom in the forests and marshes. Ducks, pheasants, herons, eagles, and many other birds build their nests in Nova Scotia. Every summer, more than one million migrating sandpipers stop in the Bay of Fundy to eat mud shrimps.

In 1901, Nova Scotia chose the mayflower for its official flower. It was the first province to have an official flower. The mayflower grows only in North America. It is a symbol of success.

Nova Scotia chose the osprey as the official bird in 1994. The osprey, or fish hawk, eats only fish. It hunts in lakes, rivers, and bays. The osprey uses its sharp **talons** to spear fish.

The Nova Scotia duck tolling retriever became the province's official dog in 1995. Often called a "duck toller," this dog was first bred in Nova Scotia in the early 1800s. It is the smallest breed of retriever.

Nova Scotia's official berry is the wild blueberry. Blueberries grow well in the province's glacial soils and mild northern climate. Nova Scotia harvests almost half of all of Canada's blueberry crop.

Nova Scotia's official tree is the red spruce. Early settlers used red spruce for building ships. This hardy tree can live up to 400 years. It is a symbol of the strength of Nova Scotia's people.

Rich in Resources

Nova Scotia's rivers and lakes provide fresh water and some **hydro-electric** power. Fishers catch cod, haddock, scallops, and lobsters from the sea. Nova Scotia exports more lobsters than any other place in the world. Water is also used for travelling in Nova Scotia. Ferries carry people and cars to New Brunswick, Newfoundland, and the United States. The Halifax harbour is Canada's busiest East Coast port. Here, huge ships deliver goods from other countries. Canadian navy ships dock in Halifax. More than 100 cruise ships call on Halifax during warmer months. About one million tourists visit the province each year.

Forests cover about 75 percent of Nova Scotia. Oak, maple, pine, and other trees make **pulp**, paper, and lumber. Nova Scotia harvests thousands of Christmas trees each year.

Nova Scotia is North America's largest producer of **gypsum**. This mineral is used to make chalk, plasterboard, and toothpaste. Nova Scotia also has large salt deposits. A mine at Pugwash produces more than 1 million tonnes of salt each year.

In 1999, Nova Scotia chose the **agate** as its official gemstone. Long ago, Aboriginal Peoples sharpened agate for tools. Today, agate is mostly used in jewellery.

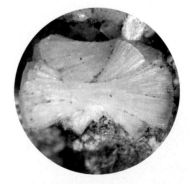

Stilbite is Nova Scotia's official mineral. Stilbite has tiny pores, or holes. The pores act like a sponge to trap odours and toxins, such as spilled oil.

Farms cover about ten percent of Nova Scotia. The Annapolis Valley and the Northumberland coastal plain grow apples for markets around the world.

Art and Culture

More than 50 museums invite people to learn about Nova Scotia's heritage and history. Nova Scotia has a greater number of historic sites than every province except Quebec. Nova Scotia also supports the arts. Halifax attracts many painters, actors, and musicians. Symphony Nova Scotia in Halifax is the only professional group of its kind in the Maritimes. Festivals and events celebrate Nova Scotia's heritage, especially Scottish culture. Every July since 1863, the Antigonish Highland Games have featured contests for athletes, Highland dancing, and bagpipe bands.

In 1956, Nova Scotia was the first province to adopt an official **tartan**. Blue and white show the sea. Green stands for forests. Red is for Scottish royalty. Gold is a symbol of Nova Scotia's ties to Great Britain.

Nova Scotia has many universities and colleges. The Gaelic College of Celtic Arts and Crafts at St. Ann's Bay is unique in North America. Students can take classes in the **Gaelic** language, Highland dancing, bagpiping, and fiddling.

Exhibits and special events celebrate African Canadian heritage at the Black Cultural Centre at Dartmouth. In Canada, February is African Heritage Month.

The Grand-Pré National Historic Site and the Acadian Museum at Chéticamp focus on the Acadian settlers in the 1700s. Today, more than 35,000 Acadians live in Nova Scotia. Acadians celebrate their French heritage with songs, music, and food.

Points of Interest

Canada created Cape Breton Highlands National Park in 1936. It was the first national park in the Maritimes. Almost half of the Cabot Trail, a scenic highway, surrounds the park. The park's 950 square kilometres of highland and coastal **habitats** protect birds and animals. Another park, the Kejimkujik National Park, covers 381 square kilometres of thick forests. The park includes a tip of the Port Mouton coast. Nova Scotia also has many forts, monuments, and old buildings that mark the province's long history.

Lunenburg shipbuilders crafted the *Bluenose* in 1921. This fishing ship won races for the next 18 years. The *Bluenose* first appeared on Canada's dime in 1937. The ship sank in 1942. Lunenburg workers built a copy of the ship in 1963, called *Bluenose II*. Today, the *Bluenose II* is Nova Scotia's official ship. It sails to many ports in Nova Scotia and the United Sates.

The Peggy's Cove lighthouse is one of Nova Scotia's top tourism sites. Nova Scotia has about 170 lighthouses, the most lighthouses of any province. The Sambro lighthouse in Nova Scotia is North America's oldest working lighthouse.

The National Historic Site of Pier 21 has been called "Canada's front door." More than one million immigrants and soldiers have passed through Halifax at Pier 21.

The current star-shaped Halifax Citadel National Historic Site was built in 1856. The Citadel held prisoners. Today, the Citadel ranks among Canada's most visited national sites.

In 1719, France began building a settlement. It is now known as Fort Louisbourg. Great Britain destroyed the fort in 1758 and took control of North America. The fort was built again in 1961 as a museum. Today, the Fort Louisbourg National Historic Site features costumed actors that show how people lived in the 1700s.

Sports and Activities

Amateur players compete in sports of all types at local schools, recreation centres, and universities. Nova Scotia does not have any major-league sports teams. However, the province has minor-league teams for sports such as hockey, rugby, and baseball. In 2006, plans began for an American League basketball team. Sports fans see many national and world sporting events in Nova Scotia. Halifax has hosted championships for hockey, figure skating, and lacrosse.

Many hockey fans believe the sport started in Nova Scotia in the late 1700s. Ice hockey came from a British stick-and-ball game called "hurley." Today, the Halifax Mooseheads play in the Quebec Major Junior Hockey League.

The province's Scottish heritage shows in Nova Scotia's sports. The Scottish games of golf and curling are common across the province.

Families enjoy camping, fishing, hiking, biking, and other outdoor summer activities at Nova Scotia's many woodland parks.

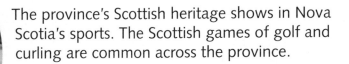

The Royal Nova Scotia International **Tattoo** hosts military teams and other performers from around the world. Teams compete in gun running, hurdles, and band competitions.

What Others Are Saying

Many people have great things to say about Nova Scotia.

Many people across Canada say phrases every day that first came from Nova Scotia's Judge Thomas Chandler Haliburton. He wrote sayings such as "raining cats and dogs" and "the early bird gets the worm."

"You can drive the length of Nova Scotia in less than a day, and nowhere are you ever more than 30 minutes from the sandy beaches, vast tidal flats or rugged cliffs of our magnificent seacoast."

"Hot, steamed lobster with drawn butter... oven-warm wild blueberry pie... creamy seafood chowders... tangy Solomon Gundy. Nova Scotia's cuisine is second to none..."

"I have traveled around the globe. I have seen the Canadian and American Rockies, the Andes, the Alps and the Highlands of Scotland, but for simple beauty Cape Breton outrivals them all."

ACTION Think about the place where you live. Come up with some words to describe your province, city, or community. Are there rolling hills and deep valleys? Can you see trees or lakes? What are some of the features of the land, people, and buildings that make your home special? Use these words to write a paragraph about the place where you live.

Test Your Knowledge

**What have you learned about Nova Scotia?
Try answering the following questions.**

1 What are some ways that people celebrate Nova Scotia's Scottish heritage?

2 Who were the first people in Nova Scotia? Where did they live? Check your library, or search on the Internet to learn more about Nova Scotia's Aboriginal Peoples.

3 The *Bluenose* made sailing history as the world's fastest fishing boat at that time. When did the *Bluenose* sink? Visit your library, or look online to learn more about shipbuilding and sailboat racing in Nova Scotia.

Create a Racing Boat

Cut a small cardboard or plastic drink carton in half. Use the bottom half for your boat. Glue coloured paper, buttons, or other decorations on your boat. Name your boat. Write a story about why you chose the boat's name. Sail the boat in your sink or bathtub.

Further Research

Books

To find out more about Nova Scotia and other Canadian provinces and territories, visit your local library. Most libraries have computers that connect to a database for researching information. If you input a key word, you will be provided with a list of books in the library that contain information on that topic. Non-fiction books are arranged numerically, using their call number. Fiction books are organized alphabetically by the author's last name.

Websites

The World Wide Web is also a good source of information. Reliable websites usually include government sites, educational sites, and online encyclopedias. Visit the following sites to learn more about Nova Scotia.

Go to the Government of Nova Scotia's website to learn about the province's government, history, and climate.
www.gov.ns.ca

Visit the Fort Louisbourg site to learn more about the province's past.
www.louisbourg.ca/fort

For information about the province, visit Explore Nova Scotia.
www.explore.gov.ns.ca

Glossary

Acadia: the name given by the French to an area that included what is now Nova Scotia

agate: a rock prized for its striped and colourful form

amateur: playing for fun, not for money or as a job

Confederation: the coming together of colonies to form the nation of Canada

dikes: barriers built to contain the flow of water or keep out the sea

fossils: parts, such as a bone, left behind by a plant or animal that lived very long ago

Gaelic: the language of Scottish highlanders

gypsum: a soft white or colourless mineral used to make cement or plaster

habitats: places where plants or animals live or grow

hydro-electric: making electricity by using the force of moving water

mace: an official staff or decorated pole that shows power or authority

pulp: a mixture of ground-up wood, rags, or other material from which paper is made

talons: sharp claws

tartan: a plaid fabric woven with designs that have special meanings

tattoo: related to the signals sounded on a drum or bugle to summon military personnel to their quarters at night

Index